Soffiati Via
Blown Away

Poems
vito m. bonito

Translated by
Allison Grimaldi Donahue

Fomite
Burlington, VT

Originally Published in Italian by: Il Ponte del Sale, Rovigo, Italy, 2015

Poems Copyright © 2021 vito m. bonito
Translation Copyright © 2021 Allison Grimaldi Donahue
Cover image: "Smoke Series" Copyright © Tiger500 2009, made available under a Creative Commons Attribution 2.0 license (https://creativecommons.org/licenses/by/2.0/)

All rights reserved. No part of this book may be reproduced in any form or by any means without the prior written consent, except in the case of brief quotations used in reviews and certain other noncommercial uses permitted by copyright law.

ISBN-13: 978-1-953236-00-5
Library of Congress Control Number: 2021947953
Fomite
58 Peru Street
Burlington, VT 05401
10-20-2021

Some poems from this collection have appeared in *The Brooklyn Rail, Exchanges University of Iowa Journal* and *Gramma Poetry Daily*. Thank you to the editors of those publications.

Thank you also to Tomás Q. Morín who was such a force of light as I worked on this translation during that winter semester at Vermont College of Fine Arts.

Contents

—*morendo/* —*dying*	3
luce eterna / eternal light	5
commedia dei fiori e della vacuità / comedy of flowers and of emptiness	25
sì dolce è il tormento / so sweet is the torment	45
antifona / antiphon	61
felicità coniugale / conjugale happiness	81
lucìe del conforto / lucias of comfort	85
bei sorrisi perduti / beautiful lost smiles	101
In the margins of *Soffiati via*	121
Translator's Note	127
About the Author	129
About the Translator	129

> The residents implored God to redeem and protect their town. God answered their prayer, he sent down an archangel who plunged the city into a fathomless lake where it survives to this day in bliss, singing their hymns and ringing bells.
>
> —Werner Herzog, *Bells from the Deep*

*Mein-
gedicht, das Genicht*
Paul Celan

*la possibilité de mourir est comme un talisman
que nous portons avec nous*
Pascal Quignard

*—morendo
si va in frantumi...*

niente buio niente barlumi

trafitture nessuno sanno...

*nessuno parla
le buie pupille
nel cielo di stelle...*

nessuno possiamo fiorire...—

*credevo volesse dire
cose che io ridire...*

*ma niente muove da un motivo
niente muore
né rimane vivo*

---

*—dying
one goes fracturing*

no dark no flickering

sharp pains no one know...

*no one speaks
dark pupils
in the sky of stars...*

no one we can make flower...—

*i thought you wanted to say
things to make me to say again...*

*but nothing moves for any reason
nothing dies
nor remains alive*

luce eterna

> *i morti "si alzano tra i morti"*
> *e recitano, come se niente fosse*
> Tadeusz Kantor

eternal light

> *the dead "awake among the dead"*
> *and act, as if it were nothing*
> Tadeusz Kantor

da bambina
seduta nel sangue
volevo sapere
cosa resta dei morti

alle manine che uccido
ora chiedo

cosa resta di me
che cosa non torna
mai più

---

as a little girl
sitting in blood
i wanted to know
what remains of the dead

to the little hands that i kill
now i ask

what of me remains
what doesn't come back
ever again

i bambini vanno morti da piccoli
come fiamme vuote
come niente
mai accaduto

i bambini stanno sognati
da chi non li ha
da chi li ha
perduti

se io non sto
sognato allora nessuno
mi ha avuto

nessuno perduto

---

the children go dead small
like empty flames
like nothing
ever happened

the children were dreamed
by those who don't have them
by those who lost
them

if i am not
dreamed so no one
had me

no one lost

i bambini hanno il cuore debole
fanno sangue le attese

nell'acqua fredda
stanno sdraiati

nell'acqua fredda
dormono senza manine

di un cuore debole
fidare non ci si può

---

children have weak hearts
waiting makes blood

in cold water
they are spread out

in cold water
they sleep without little hands

a weak heart
one cannot trust it

voglio che sia sepolta
col vestitino da sposa

non provate a riaccenderla

il vento non torna

---

i want her buried
in a little wedding dress

don't try to relight her

the wind won't return

deve accadere

dove niente
senza dolore

ma non finire

dove niente
arde il fiore

poi
scende il cuore

il latte di mamma
bevilo ancora

scioglici dentro
promesse d'amore

le tue caramelle di sangue

---

it has to happen

where nothing
without pain

but don't finish

where nothing
ignites the flower

then
the heart comes down

mother's milk
keep drinking it

melt inside
promises of love

your caramels of blood

bambini fioriscono i cani

angelico aleggia il bastone
i cani
si fa il sapone

i cani accarezzati

sulla barchetta
bambini cromati

al guinzaglio

beati

---

children flower dogs

angelic the cane flutters
the dogs
you make soap

the coddled dogs

on the small boat
chrome-plated babies

on the leash

blessed

i grandi fanno bambini-didentro
troppo piccoli

così loro-didentro
muoiono
troppo presto

nessuno è mai abbastanza
grande
da rimanere vivo

---

grown-ups make babies-thereinside
too much little ones

so they-thereinside
die
too soon

no one is ever big
enough
to stay alive

le persone piccole di sangue
respirano male

fiori vivi
senz'aria

il sole li trema
fino alla fine

mehr licht
mehr nicht

---

little people of blood
breathe badly

flowers alive
without air

the sun shakes them
all the way to the end

mehr licht
mehr nicht

così nasci
la prima volta

se vendi il sangue

così puoi restare
viva

tenere in braccio
i tuoi capelli

---

like this you're born
the first time

if you sell your blood

like this you can stay
alive

hold it in your arms
your hair

si è chiusa nel silenzio

non hanno sofferto

guarda le mani
guardale senza

in cielo si va
un poco alla volta

---

closed in silence

they didn't suffer

look at the hands
look at them without

one goes into the sky
a little at a time

sono le persone col didentro di sangue
che ci nascono

e poi ci muoiono piatte
che usciamo da noi

nel mondo della polvere trasparente
le bambole di carta
si tengono per mano

---

there are people with thereinsides of blood
that we are born from

and then they die us flat
so we come out of us

in the world of transparent dust
the paper dolls
hold each other's hands

sono arrivati gli occhi!

ora mi prendo la morte
e vedo
le voci elettriche

non importa più
quanto io creda nella salvezza

le statuine
si sono svegliate

---

the eyes have arrived!

now i take up death
and i see
electric voices

it no longer matters
how much i believe in release

the statuettes
have awoken

mi hanno messo a crescere dentro
nella pancia viva un bambino

mi hanno detto
non devi mangiare
lo uovo-bambino

le cose che mancano dentro
lo uovo si rompe

l'odore degli angeli fa
e non si può usare

non devono uscire
dalla testa
         i colori

---

they put me to grow inside
a baby in the living belly

to me they said
you don't have to eat
the egg-baby

the things missing inside
the egg breaks

makes the smell of angels
and you can't use it

they mustn't come out
from the head
         the colors

uno dei miei bambini
si è ucciso senza ragione

ovvero da qualche parte
senza ragione
la luce ha trovato più spazio

---

one of my babies
killed herself for no reason

i mean somewhere
for no reason
the light found more space

escono dalle fiamme
ridono ardono

si passano l'aria
le stelle
sudano il cuore fiorito

cosa vediamo noi
quando
non vediamo più niente

niente sta nel fuoco
la cenere mente

---

they come out of flames
they laugh they burn

they pass through air
the stars
they sweat the flowered heart

what do we see
when
we no longer see anything

nothing is in the fire
the ash lies

il corpo del bambino non bastava

le statuine di sangue
dondolano il cielo

rifiutano il cibo
innamorate

bevono
luce eterna
dalle costole

adorate

---

the child's body wasn't enough

the statuettes of blood
wobble the sky

they refuse food
in love

they drink
eternal light
from the ribs

worshipped

sono riapparsi
i bambini cromati

ogni uno ha fatto preghiera
ogni uno ha fatto luce
ogni uno lo stomaco pulito

ora tutti
possiamo
uccidere
tutti

---

they've reappeared
the chrome-plated babies

each one said prayers
each one made light
each one clean stomach

now everyone
we can
kill
everyone

non enterai dice la pietra
ti manca il respiro

ogni respiro
ti ha rifiutato

―――――――――――――――――――

you will not enter says the stone
you lack breath

every breath
has refused you

la mia infanzia fu triste
come un sudario

allora mi sposerò per avere
molti bambini

vedi quella foto?

è iddio
quando sono morta

---

my childhood was sad
like a shroud

so i will marry to have
many children

see that photo?

it is mygod
when i died

**commedia dei fiori
e della vacuità**

> *si attacano alla pelle, questi fiori,
> lasciano ferite, ferite incurabili*
> Mariella Mehr

**comedy of flowers
and of emptiness**

> *they stick to the skin, these flowers
> leave wounds, incurable wounds*
> Mariella Mehr

I

le vere persone diluite
avvengono all'alba

fanno a pioggia
i respiri

cadono a mille
dal cielo
a scintille

I

the real diluted people
emerge at sunrise

like rain
take breaths

they fall a flood
from the sky
sparkling

II

le astrazioni non ti salveranno

iddio ha detto

i pesci brillano di luce propria

non dormono

non hanno occhi

II

abstractions will not save you

mygod said

fish shine from their own light

they don't sleep

have no eyes

III

i fiorellini nel prato
all'infinito
respirano insieme

la benzina
apre la fame mattutina

il digiuno fa sognare
cani e bambini
sull'altare

III

the little flowers in the field
to infinity
breathe together

the gasoline
opens the morning hunger

fasting makes dreams
dogs and babies
on the altar

IV

che tu sia lodato
a schegge a tremore

nel vuoto più nero
del fiore

IV

that you are praised
in tremoring shards

in the blackest emptiness
of the flower

V

il padre spesso
le accompagnava
al cimitero

bisbiglianti figurine
bestie
       divine

V

the father often
accompanied them
to the cemetery

murmuring figurines
beasts
       divine

VI

usa il coltello
comincia da sinistra
la gola è perfetta

mantieni la promessa
tienimi per mano

VI

use the knife
start from the left
the throat is perfect

hold to the promise
hold my hand

VII

io non ho mani

iddio crescere fammi
             le mani

VII

i don't have hands

mygod grow them i demand
                    hands

VIII

alla luce
eterna ogni bocca
si apre

siamo malati

siamo
bellissimi

VIII

at the light
eternal every mouth
opens

we are sick

we are
so beautiful

IX

ora che sono morto
iddio si piega
e respira come un cane
nel sangue s'annida
nella fame

come un resto
senza conforto

un miracolo storto
un bisbiglio lontano

IX

now that i'm dead
mygod stoops
and breathes like a dog
in blood he nuzzles
in hunger

like a rest
without respite

a crooked miracle
a distant murmur

X

gli uccellini del freddo
scendono i morti
a mangiare

ognuno l'altro battezza

nel sangue
si rotola

lucia

X

the little birds of the cold
bring down the dead
to eat

each baptizes the other

in blood
they roll

lucia

XI

mettiti freddi i vestitini
non torneranno i lumini

le vedi le statuine?
vacillano appena
come i bambini

smonta i corpicini
mangia gli ossicini

XI

put on your little clothes cold
candles won't come back

see the statuettes
they teeter just so
like babies

disassemble the little bodies
eat the little bones

XII

persi nel diluvio

vedono solo
voci nel vento

alberi bianchi
nel firmamento

XII

lost in the flood

they only see
voices in the wind

white trees
in the firmament

XIII

hanno rami
come mani

implorano
l'ardore
senza fine

la fiamma
ossidrica è qui

in lacrime già
nel suo fiore

XIII

they have branches
like hands

they implore
the heat
without end

the flame
thrower is here

in tears already
in its flower

XIV

non guardare nel vento

le anime sono svanite

i bambini sottili
se le sono fumate

XIV

don't look in the wind

the souls have vanished

the frail babies
smoked them

XV

a volte succede che mi taglio le mani
comincia che parlo due cuori
lontani

la mente segretamente comprende
che l'orrore è la mente allora
mi taglio le mani e tutto comincia io dico
tutte le vite quante vissute
e poi morte le vite ottenute
io dico quante
vite finite quali respiri dietro la luce
perduti

la pietà non ha peso
la pietà non ha peso io peso
grammi ventuno
dentro le mani
arrese
la vita resa io dico

il cielo e nulla qui non c'è nulla
io dico e parlo e non dico il cuore lontano
che spàlpita e sta nella mano

fino a quando si muore? quante vite si muore
quando l'anima esplode e si spoglia e tutto
cominicia? tutta del corpo la cenere
e il male e poi senza peso
tutto cade imporando e si spegne
e poi tutto cominicia
luce ancora di sangue
dal cuore irradiate
senza perdono vaghissime mani

XV

sometimes it happens that i cut my hands
it begins that i speak two hearts
distant

the mind secretly understands
that the horror is the mind so
i cut my hands and it all begins i say
all the lives how many lived
and then dead the lives obtained
i say how many
lives ended which breaths behind the light
lost

compassion has no weight
compassion has no weight i weigh
grams twenty-one
inside the hands
surrendered
life surrendered i tell you

the sky and nothing here there is nothing
i tell and speak and i don't tell the distant heart
that sputters and sits in the hand

until when do you die? how many lives do you die
when the soul explodes and undresses and everything
begins? all the body ash
and the pain and then without weight
it all falls imploring and turns off
and then it all begins
light still of blood
from the radiated heart
without forgiveness vague hands

e poi nessuno e nessuna grammatica
e nessunluogo e niente e nessungrammo
quanto pesa un fiato di vento
un resto bruciato e sgomento
allora tutto cade allora mi taglio le mani
così cercano il cuore
e poi il cuore senza ricresce le mani
e le mani il cuore dentro ricrescono
quasi ventuno
gridi quasi mani
cuori smaniati
se l'anima appena
quale schianto
il peso di grammi ventuno soffiato
via solo perché mi scuori e mi smani
e mi svesti di carne
e di pelle mi lasci soltanto

anima viola a sonagli
nell'ombra di sangue
quanto perduto
va quanto
a non essere sangue
si sogna

quante morte mani quante
vite quante vanno quanti cuori
sussurrano vivi alla pioggia
e cadono cadono
senzavento lontani

ventuno
grammi
ventuno

nessuno

and then no one and no grammar
and noplace and nothing and nograms
how much does a breath of wind weigh
a buried dismayed relic
so everything falls so i cut off my hands
like this they search for the heart
and then the heart regenerated without the hands
and the hands the heart inside regenerate
almost twenty-one
cries almost hands
yearning hearts
the soul barely
which pang
the weight of twenty-one grams blown
away only because you rip out my heart and hands
and you strip me of flesh
and you leave me only skin

violet soul rattles
in the shadow of blood
how much lost
so much
it is no longer blood
one dreams

how many dead hands how many
lives how many go how many hearts
murmur alive like rain
and fall fall
withoutwind distant

twenty-one
grams
twenty-one

no one

sì dolce è il tormento

si è volatilizzato come la canfora
Tadeusz Kantor

niente è reale
niente è certo
difficile dire…
Werner Herzog

so sweet is the torment

it volatized like camphor
Tadeusz Kantor

nothing is real
nothing is certain
difficult to say…
Werner Herzog

I

[…]

conservata sotto vetro
è viva ogni cosa

nato appena
ogni essere umano
deve prendere fuoco

tornare increato

[…]

ancora
mentre morire nel cielo

guardami tra i volati
guardami
tra i non pensati

[…]

niente commuovere i sensi
né cielo cadere dove moriamo
ora materia
sola come sempre già stati
ancora finire
nascere
sotto stelle mai vive

[…]

se dovrà soffrire
se dovrà soffrire

ogni cosa
sola
nel sangue

I

[…]

preserved under glass
every thing lives

just born
each human being
must catch on fire

to return uncreated

[…]

still
while to die in the sky

watch me among the flying
watch me
watch me among the not-thought-ofs

[…]

nothing moves the senses
nor sky to fall where we die
now material
alone as always already been
yet to finish
to be born
under never living stars

[…]

if there must be suffering
if there must be suffering

each thing
alone
in blood

[…]

pause chiarori fumi
da lungo tempo
                tremori

chiarori se pure non fosse
mai nato chiarori se nato
vaga pausa di vita

[…]

in fiamme perché
creato
perché non tardi
a morire
ad uscire dal lume
finito lume
se nato

[…]

quel giorno dira libido
dira dulcedo dell'ira

iddio segna i nati
iddio sogna tu sogni
iddio segna
la luce tu guardi
la luce

io guardo la mia
luce morire

[…]

quasi trèmiti trèmiti
mai altri occhi

è questo il mio altare?

[...]

pauses dim smokes
for a long time
               tremors

dim even if there were none
never born dim if born
vague pause of life

[...]

in flames because
created
because not late
to die
to leave from the glow
finished glow
if born

[...]

that day dira libido
dira dulcedo of ire

mygod marks the born
mygod dreams your dreams
mygod marks
the light you watch
the light

i watch my
light to die

[...]

nearly tremors tremors
never other eyes

is this my altar?

i fiori morti dentro i vivi

[…]

le manine al cuore
inchiodate
ancora fino alla fine
cercare conforto
ancora

[…]

ma quasi nei sangui
assopito sognando
dolore
　　　　insaziabile

[…]

sangue illumina i sogni
luce su luce ogni volato
s'accende arde s'infuoca
òrbita sfiata ricorda

[…]

mi sono fatto un corpo
mutilato

l'ho messo a fuoco

la vita cerca la vita

[…]

oh manina oh mia
vagina
fiore scuoiato
capra chimera
ingenerata
soffiami seme

the dead flowers inside the living

[...]

the little hands at the heart
nailed
still until the end
to search for comfort
still

[...]

but almost in bloods
dozed off dreaming
pain
                insatiable

[...]

blood illuminates dreams
light on light each flying
ignites burns sets ablaze
orbits deflates remembers

[...]

i made myself a body
mutilated

i set it on fire

life searches for life

[...]

oh little hands oh my
vagina
skinned flower
goat chimera
generated
blow me seed

prima agognato
poi avvelenato

portami a nanna
nel sonno dei cani

portami all'ira
sorridimi sangue

[…]

termine fisso di ogni tuo figlio
ultimo sogno cometa
in notte vacua di stelle

dàgli disprezzo
nàscilo aperta ferita
nàscilo cieco
chiamalo vita

dei nati ira vertita

—io nel sangue ti prego
fioriscimi uccidimi—

first longed for
then poisoned

carrying me to beddy-bye
in the sleep of dogs

carry me to ire
smile me blood

[…]

fixed time for each of your sons
last dream comet
in night vacuous of stars

give him disdain
birth him open wound
birth him blind
call him life

of the born ire vertita

—i in the blood beg you
flower me kill me—

II

[…]

ogni secondo tremila stelle
si uccidono

[…]

io non so misurare la pausa
tra il rumore della mente
e il suo orrore

[…]

sto in pensiero
come dire sto in sospeso
come dire ogni bestia tace
come dire lettera morta

[…]

un calcio nella pancia
il primo rumore
sangue del primo amore
io dietro la nuca
fuori respiro

[…]

bestia in fuga percossa
nel sangue
sotto stelle di sangue
senza voce
lettera morta già morta

II

[…]

every second three thousand stars
kill themselves

[…]

i do not know how to measure the pause
between the sound of the mind
and its horror

[…]

i am in thought
as to say i am suspended
as to say every beast quiets
as to say the dead letter

[…]

a kick in the belly
the first sound
blood of the first love
i behind the nape
outside breathe

[…]

beast in flight bruised
in blood
under the stars of blood
voiceless
dead letter already dead

[…]

da quel momento sto in pensiero
sento il sangue in ogni stanza
lentissimo

da quel momento
ho cominciato sangue
a cantare

[…]

se uccidere potessi il bambino
gli toglierei il respiro
la sua vocina spegnersi
fino a sentire

vedere la sua
boccuccia che sbatte
nel vuoto

ora dillo vocina
—sono io sono qui—

se un pesciolino fosse
in acqua lo rimetterei

un pesciolino non è

[…]

due
uccidere
volevo uccidere
bambini
due

[…]

from the moment i am in thought
i feel blood in every room
so slow

from that moment
i began blood
to sing

[…]

if i could kill the baby
i would take the breath
shut off his little voice
until feeling

to see his
little mouth that beats
in the emptiness

now tell him little voice
—i am me i am here—

if he were a little fish
in water i'd return him

a little fish he isn't

[…]

two
to kill
i wanted to kill
babies
two

poi

nessuno soffrire
ho detto

uno
allora ucciso

uno

[…]

cantare—
sangue fare

then

no one said to suffer
i said

one
so killed

one

[…]

to sing —
blood to make

antifona

antiphon

zero è il nostro iddio

vetro filato
a sangue nel sorriso

rosa del dove senza cosa

mangiare
morire
poi digerire

siamo sazie
cantiamo

l'alveare
finalmente ci appare

---

zero is our my god

barbed glass
with blood in the smile

rose of where without the thing

eat
die
then digest

we are satisfied
we sing

the beehive
finally appears to us

arse dove respiriamo
senza conoscere o ricordare

fumano i sangui
noi la testa
 tintinnando

---

burned where we breathe
without knowing or remembering

the bloods smoke
we the head
 ringing

nostra luce
opaca e nostra

chi rimane cosa rimane

più pura umana
cosa

benedizione
selezione
soluzione
salvezza
macellazione

---

our light
opaque and ours

who remains what remains

purest human
thing

benediction
selection
solution
salvation
butchery

piccolo cranio diluvio
primavera di ombre

aprirsi fiorire morire
appena tremore

favole
focolai

fino alla fine

---

little skull flood
spring of shadows

open up flower die
barely a tremor

fairy tales
breeding grounds

until the very end

chiome sangue comete
vaghissime voci

come bocche lasciate al delirio

in ginocchio perdute
in lacrime

umane

fiammelle

---

hair blood comets
echoing voices

like mouths left to delirium

on knees lost
in tears

humans

tiny flames

nessuna dimora nessuna
pausa incisioni

apparizioni

lontane
umane
vane

---

no dwelling no
pause incisions

apparitions

distant
human
idle

cenere quasi dopo
quasi gridi
quanti

quasi cenere viola
dentro i gridi

cenere quasi animule
quasi a comete

discendono
soffiano sfiatano

habeas corpus
nostro infinito svanire

---

ashes almost after
almost shouts
how many

almost violet ashes
inside the shouts

ashes almost little souls
almost like comets

they descend
they blow they deflate

habeas corpus
our infinity to disappear

appena fessure
impulsi
ora deboli
ora sognati

più gridi
da quando erano stati

fredde piume
chioma di sangue

---

barely a fissure
impulses
now weak
now dreamed

more cries
from when they were

cold feathers
mane of blood

questo è un viaggio di ritorno
la parte incompiuta
di un già dato oltrepassare

questo è un viaggio
che non torna
non sente più l'andare

venire a galla
è solo altro sognare

e poi dovunque
muto soffocare

---

this is a return trip
the unfinished part
that's already been trespassed

this is a trip
that has no return
doesn't feel like going further

to come to the surface
is only another way to dream

and everywhere
mute suffocation

come hai voluto
è niente

essere qui è capitato
essere qui sangue versato

in ginocchio
nel buio

dove mai ogni stella

---

as you wanted
it is nothing

to be here happened
to be here blood spilled

on knees
in the dark

where never every star

io sono vivo perché
c'ho il fuoco dentro la testa
e anche i cani
senz'occhi
vengono e vanno
nel fuoco
dentro la testa

iddio balbettano
chi siamo non sa
né cosa vogliamo

ardere vivi
è cosa
buona e giusta quel tanto
che di noi fa
cenere a stento

ronzio
della nostra empietà

---

i am alive because
i have fire inside my head
also dogs
without eyes
come and go
in the fire
inside my head

mygod they stutter
who we are don't know
nor what we want

to burn alive
is something
good and rightous
that to turn us
ashes is tough

buzz
with our evil

si finisce poi
che a vivere
si ha paura

si finisce poi
che si appare in sogno
si dicono cose che i vivi
senso non hanno
e poi fanno insonnia
fanno terrore di prendere
sonno

fa sperare
dormire

a dormire
si finisce
impazziti

---

you finish then
that to live
you are afraid

you finish then
that you appear in dreams
saying things that the living
make no sense
and then cause insomnia
make terror to fall
asleep

make you hope
sleep

sleeping
you end up
crazed

allora una
due tre
quattro solo tre
al bisogno
massimo quattro

in cauda miniàs non pregare
cinque non dire
dimentica l'aria
arrenditi all'ira

quattro ogni notte
sempre ogni notte
pediatrica dose
pediatrica morte

---

so one
two three
four only three
as needed
maximum four

in cauda miniàs do not pray
five don't say
forget the air
surrender to ire

four every night
always every night
pediatric dose
pediatric death

giochiamo che torno
in clinica solo domani

per stanotte
         dormo

giochiamo che mai
ottobre novembre
gennaio dicembre
ma solo settembre
agosto e il 31 dicembre

giochiamo che più non ho i denti
così non scendono lacrime
che gli occhi non perdo
e mi taglio le mani

giochiamo che cadi
nel sonno infinita
come il cuore s'annienta
al respiro caduto nel fiore

che nessuno mi aiuta
a morire giochiamo

che io
         muoio
sono morto
ora e ti annuso

tra gli alberi a sangue

che non te ne vai

let's play that i go back
to the clinic only tomorrow

for tonight
         i sleep

let's play that never
october november
january december
but only september
august and the 31st of december

let's play that i haven't got teeth anymore
that way tears don't come down
that i don't lose my eyes
and i cut off my hands

let's play that you fall
into infinite sleep
like the heart annihilates itself
for the breath fallen in the flower

that no one helps me
we play at dying

that i
        die
i am dead
now and i sniff you

amongst the trees of blood

that you don't run away

pace ordine tranquillità—
il corpo vive

io penso io vivo—
il male esiste

---

peace order tranquility—
the body lives

i think i live—
evil exists

te lucis ante…
occhi persi all'improvviso

me tra luci sante
sì… l'inferno il paradiso

me tra lingue spente
me che me ne vado
                nella mente

---

te lucis ante…
eyes lost suddenly

me among sacred lights
yes… hell heaven

me among tired tongues
me who runs off
                in the mind

felicità coniugale

conjugale happiness

mai fu stella al suo spegnersi più pura
Giovanni Giudici

never was a star in its vanishing more pure
Giovanni Giudici

mamma
che lavoro fa
iddio?

— prosciuga le anime —

...

iddio
che lavoro fa
mamma?

— mangia i resti —

*

è un pesce
mia madre

senz'occhi

...

sotto spirito

mio padre
nessuno lo vede

*

oh mio sogno fetale

unica mia
porta fecale

*mommy
what work does
mygod work at?*

— dries up souls —

…

*mygod
what work does
mommy work at?*

— eats the remains —

*

*she's a fish
my mommy*

without eyes

…

under spirit

*my father
no one sees him*

*

oh my fetal dream

*only mine
fecal doorway*

lucìe del conforto

> *tutto si divide in se stesso*
> Samuel Beckett

lucias of comfort

> *everything divides in itself*
> Samuel Beckett

l'albero mi ha parlato
ma io non sapevo
parlare la lingua

allora mi sono inciso
così ho parlato
il mio sangue

---

the tree spoke to me
but i didn't know
to speak the language

so i cut myself
that way i spoke
my blood

morire di fame non basta

così mi sono data
in pasto alle sanguisughe

nessuno si redime
senza darsi in pasto
alle sanguisughe

---

to die of hunger isn't enough

so i give myself up
as chum to the leeches

no one redeems himself
without giving himself up as chum
to the leeches

io conosco le cose
che hanno paura
perciò voglio essere
inciso

per essere inciso
devo toccare
le vespe di iddio

dentro i fiori morti
devo parlare
più luminoso

---

i know the things
that are afraid
for that i want to be
cut

to be cut
i must touch
the wasps of mygod

inside dead flowers
i must speak
more luminous

molti alberi hanno il cancro
molti uccelli non vedono
più

il resto non conta

è solo luce

filo spinato

---

many trees have cancer
many birds don't see
anymore

the rest doesn't count

it is only light

barbed wire

si deforma
tutta la vita

iddio mi sorride

finalmente
mi dice

— respira

io devo avere
tu devi dare —

---

you deform
your entire life

mygod smiles at me

finally
says to me

— breathe

i must have
you must give —

un velo liquido
fino all'estasi

trafitta
confusa

brace umana

superinfusa

---

a liquid veil
until ecstasy

pierced
confused

human embers

overinfused

la grazia intorno
a me la grazia

i bambini di polvere
mettono a fuoco
tutti i gradi della perfezione

una volta le culle
cantavano in coro

la luce splendeva

dentro il fuoco
io ero vivo

---

the grace surrounding
to me grace

the children of dust
set to flames
all degrees of perfection

once the cradles
sang in chorus

the light gleamed

inside the fire
i was alive

dopo aver aspirato l'aria
i bambini di polvere
dichiararono
l'epoca della giustizia trionfante

il buio si riempiva di sussurri
farà male? farà male?

---

after having inhaled the air
the children of dust
declared
the epoch of triumphant justice

the darkness fills with whispers
will it hurt? will it hurt?

i senzamani
ci danno la comunione

pregano fuoco

la mutilazione
è un gioco

---

the withouthands
give us communion

they pray fire

the mutilation
is a game

è stata semplicemente una festa
andata a finire male

le bestie ammansite
si sono date allo sbrano

non bastarono le lenzuola
a coprire i resti
di corpi anime e cenere
in volo

pietosa la neve discese
a farsi gloria di sangue

ultimo velo

---

it was simply a party
that ended badly

the curbed beasts
tore each other to pieces

the sheets are not enough
to cover the remains
of bodies souls and ashes
in the air

merciful the snow falls
to make glory of blood

last veil

disattesa la speranza
che già tutti morti

è primavera
ogni dolore
nel vuoto

così sia

---

hope disregarded
that already all dead

it is spring
every pain
in the emptiness

so be it

finisce il mondo
se non riprendi
a tremare

finisce il mondo
se continui
a respirare

---

the world ends
if you don't get back
to quiver

the world ends
if you continue
to breathe

non è se ragionare sanno
né se parlare

la domanda è se
possono
soffrire

[…]

fai luce
ad una spegni
ad una le ombre
giocattolo

---

it is not if they can reason
nor if they can speak

the question is if
they can
suffer

[…]

you make light
at one you switch off
at one the shadows
toy

l'albero ha mangiato il cuore

nessun animale
ha voluto avvicinarsi

l'albero si è spento

---

the tree ate the heart

no animal
wanted to come close

the tree switched off

bei sorrisi perduti

dio non zoppica
G.H.

beautiful lost smiles

god doesn't limp
G.H.

si fanno le convulsioni

nei reni che iddio
dentro ci sfiata

---

convulsions occur

in the kidneys that mygod
deflates in there

io conto le stelle con gli alberi
ogni ramo
appendo un bambino

un cielo di corpi
un bosco di luci

[…]

questa
è la mia pace

---

i count the stars with the trees
every branch
i hang a baby

a sky of bodies
a forest of lights

[…]

this
is my peace

brulicano
i bambini lumaca
dentro l'elettricità

le bambole vive
non strisciano più

le api le api
l'eternità

---

they swarm
the babies snail
inside the electricity

the living dolls
no longer slither

the bees the bees
eternity

io sono buio
dice un bambino

ogni mattina
nella gioia mi uccido

---

i am darkness
says a child

every morning
in the joy i kill myself

iddio mi ha ordinato
di non camminare
non masticare

di non spargere olio
santo sul cranio bruciato

[…]

iddio mi ha ordinato
di bere fuoco

ma solo quello dei malati
e delle stelle morenti

[…]

iddio mi ordinato
di seppellirmi

vivo
e di non morire

---

mygod ordered me
not to walk
not to chew

not to spread holy
oil on the burned skull

[…]

mygod ordered me
to drink fire

but only that of the sick
and of the dying stars

mygod ordered me
to bury myself

alive
and not to die

scendono le bambine di neve
scendono in luce perpetua

lo sai nessuna manina
ci tiene la tua
lo sai c'è chi muore per noi
e fiorisce sugli occhi la bua

scendono cieche
le bambine di neve
la pelle a sonagli
è un mantello di fame

bambino dicono puoi
sorridere fiori per te
non abbiamo

non è il tuo dolore il dolore
di questo mondo cosa non è

ardono i rami cadono stelle
la nostra vita non conta più niente
la nostra vita è un respiro olocausto

bevi il sangue
il sangue non mente

il cielo è tutto per te

they come down the snow babies
they come down in perpetual light

you know no little hand
holds yours
you know that there's who dies for us
and flowers on the eyes the boo-boo

they come down blind
the snow babies
the skin with a rattle
is a coat of hunger

baby they say you can
to laugh flowers for you
we do not have

the pain is not your pain
of this world what is not

the branches they burn stars fall
our life no longer counts for anything
our life is a holocaustal breath

drink the blood
the blood doesn't lie

the sky is all for you

adorate mie vespe
dove andate
adorate stelline?

la dolcezza vi chiama
del sacrificio carnale?

forse che si avvicina
la bambina senz'occhi?

---

my worshipped wasps
where do you go
worshipped little stars?

sweetness calls you
of the carnal sacrifice?

maybe that she moves close
the child without eyes?

nostro puro essere qui
infuse lanterne

nel vetro iniettate
umane ombre illuse

scintille del niente

nel mai finito ruotare

---

our pure being here
infused lanterns

in injected glass
deluded human shadows

glints of nothing

in the never finished revolve

mi avevi detto
che non morivamo

ma la luce ci apre

ci fa sottili sottili
in ginocchio

come gli angeli
come la carta

---

you had told me
that we didn't die

but the light opens us

makes us thin thin
on knees

like angels
like paper

malati anime belle
miei cari bambini

qui si digiuna nel fuoco
girando nel buio
e nel vuoto

iddio credetemi è un forno

d'oro che dentro ci sta
il sangue con tutte le stelle

---

sick beautiful souls
my dear children

here you fast in the fire
wandering in the dark
in the emptiness

mygod believe me it is an oven

of gold that has inside
blood with all the stars

nel nuovo secolo
diventeremo
tutti pazzi

ci saranno mille milioni
di bambini felici

forme pure
gabbie per uccelli morenti

---

in the new century
we will become
all of us crazy

there will be a thousand millions
of happy children

pure forms
cages of dying birds

a volte
sono vuota
per un tempo lunghissimo

mi chiamo lucia

aiuto i bambini
a morire

---

on occasion
i am empty
for a long long time

my name is lucia

i help the children
to die

che bello
è arrivato natale

ecco la nostra
ossidrica fiamma

dono
consustanziale

noi dentro a bruciare
la nostra parvenza vitale

sia detto
non c'è paradiso

più bello
di questo sorriso

---

how beautiful
the day of birth has arrived

here is our
flame thrower

offering
consubstantial

us inside to burn
our trace of life

may be said
there is no paradise

more beautiful
than this smile

la testa ci svuota
ombre scavare

—*vieni ha me*
se sei stanca
io ti vacillerò—

---

the head empties
shadows to excavate

—*come have me*
if you are tired
i will sway you—

non ho mai dato un bacio

ho nove anni

domani mi bruciano

viva

---

i have never given a kiss

i am nine years old

tomorrow they burn me

alive

In the margins of *Soffiati via*

Soffiati via is a book that, for many years, remained dormant and underground. It couldn't find its language; it wasn't able to take the shape it would eventually inhabit.

A kind of language forgotten to itself – and to the place from which it is pronounced. The multiplication of voices and figures that populate the space has thwarted every attempt to grant a perceptive and singular centrality to the structure of the book. It is an exploded and bewildered book that is literally neither in Heaven nor on Earth, just as the bodies and souls that pass through it are not in Heaven nor on Earth either.

The problem, for me, was to confront the fear of saying things that only children, or serial killers, or the most hideous lowlife of humanity, are capable of expressing.

The only way to perceive or restore these chasms was to forget my language, or that which I believed was my language, and its selective and censorial power. In this way I have dedicated and decorated a paradise without a center and without the paradisiacal: as it opens in up the gaze and in the words of those who kill and those who are killed.

*

I believe that the formal or syntactic infractions that had already manifested in *Fioritura del sanguine* (Roma, Perrone, 2010) and again in the blind obsession with rhyme in *fabula rasa* (Salerno, Oèdipus, 2018) are real interferences, distortions, due to the distance from which the word and its sound come. A distance without direction from which mesmerically, hypnotically, come the making and undoing of language and the logical micro-collapses of speech. It would be like photographing spirits and trying to shape borderless shadows.

*

That childhood is linked to pain and death is evident to me - as is its crippled chant. Getting out of childhood or out of life is the same thing. Childhood, then, has a cruelty and a truth that kill.

Since becoming a father (and already saying father kills me) I have discovered the ferocious and sweet irony that children (even in simple babbling) carry within themselves.

*

If I had to name books or authors who have continuously marked my poetry, I would invoke the Old Testament, Dante, and Beckett, but I would also have to summon Therese of Lisieux, Sophocles, Celan, Caproni, Dostoevskji, Pascoli, Cioran, Wallace Stevens, Thomas Bernhard, Mandelstam, Achmatova, the theater of the Socìetas Raffaello Sanzio, Werner Herzog.

Then, each of my books has its own story. There are novels, essays on philosophy and art history that have given me verses, entire poems. A while ago I rediscovered Franco Fortini, for example. I like his epigrammatic poetry, his ferocity, the blind moralistic hatred from which there is no respite. This also applies to Brecht. I admire them - and read them backwards and forwards. Like grafting them into a disturbed writing - or even better thinking that they are opera librettists. And indeed, writing librettos was a youthful passion to which I have returned. It gives me the possibility of a parodying instrumentation, of a falsetto counterpoint.

*

One writes already dead.

One writes to the dead, to the not-born. It is only this that I sought to do and what I seek to do.

Whoever writes gives himself to death in language and listens to language while he dies.

Book after book, within this trauma, in the fire of the original scene, mine of course, which is being born to death. Thus, one approaches the void of the voice, the fragile infallibility of being nothing.

In my last two books (*Soffiati via* and *fabula rasa*) this path almost naturally led to the pataphysical overthrow, to the melopoeia, to the sacrificial liturgy, to the crippled and suffocated song.

"The end is in the beginning and yet you go on," Hamm would tell us, in Beckett's *Endgame*. With him, all of Beckett's voices teach us that the words of those characters come from those who cannot understand that they are neither alive nor dead. Those characters, those voices - wrote Emil Cioran - "have jumped from birth to agony, without transitions, without existence: human waste that no longer has anything to learn or to deal with, who mull over - hilarious or amazed - about futility and that from time to time they throw some lightning out of contempt, some oracle. We understand them only if we admit that something has irremediably broken, concluded, that they belong not to the end of history but to what comes after, to that perhaps imminent, perhaps distant future, in which the shrinking of man will reach the perfection of an overturned utopia."

The ending of *Soffiati via* serves as an exemplary text: four lines, a farewell to no one, within a condemnation that is close by, but already in place, while the text unfolds:

i have never given a kiss

i am nine years old

tomorrow they burn me

alive

A little girl speaks of being burned alive. Is it a sacrifice? Punishment for her guilt? An execution for no reason? An act of pure cruelty that has no horizon of understanding? Like all the texts in the book, this one also makes no sense. Neither first nor last. It does not refer to a beginning or an end. It is a sudden gust of wind that blows out a candle ("blown away" remains one of the possible and least unfaithful meanings of the word nirvāna. Every extinction happens just as every birth happens. It is delivered to the world or nothing. It lights up and goes out): to close a series of slim lives or non-lives, of childhoods already tortured, raped, skinned. A chorus of not-born, neither alive, nor dead.

So it is, but it is not so; or it is not only. The book opens where the voices declare that nothing dies or stays alive. Everything is or should be inside this opaque light.

Yet these neither living nor dead act, they acted within a glint of blood. By will and by destiny, by necessity.

The initial intention of the book was to tell the mind and deeds of a serial killer, who later became a homicidal child.

In doing so, the book took a different turn: every act of will, even when sick, of someone dissolved in the blind movement of the unexpected that happens.

Everything that happens just happens. It does not arise from a decision to be trusted; it does not die in the fulfillment of this decision. It just happens, just like poetry happens.

The problem (or the gamble) is not to flinch from the horror of pain without direction, not to stop looking, not to stop speaking. These are the few essential things a writer should, must, do.

All my poetic experience and (why not) my more or less normal biography revolve around this very simple matter, around this studded horizon. Do not retreat, do not cover your eyes and ears in front of and within the trauma, do not hide from the facts and words we possess and those we are unable to possess.

Things happen, words must happen; they must possibly fall - to the end, to an end.

Up until one's blatant failure, up until not being able to say.

The poetic act is a happy evil that one cannot do without, an embellishment of blood that never ceases writing itself.

If it didn't seem too sentimental, I would say it borders on blind hatred, rancor without reason. Pure hate. Absolute resentment that grants no peace and does not know why, offers no because. Pure hatred, gratuitous and objectless rancor (like the most blind and deaf love) produce extraordinary visions, enchanting contagions from which poetry must not escape, nor can it escape.

You just have to find the words, the exact order of the *verba* inoculated with hate - or god.

Poetry like hatred neither loves nor admits mistakes, but somehow compassionately contemplates them, where every book is unfinished, never finished, forever failed. Where it turns over in prayer, litany, lullaby.

Like poetry, hatred needs to fail and continually move.

Like how poetry is viral and not virtual.

Soffiati via wanted to stay in this fold. Among the neither living nor dead, words open to an order (and also to a command, a commandment) to which one can respond in the only way one can - here I am. To hear is nothing other than to obey.

*

Poetry is the acoustic dramaturgy of distance, syncope, spasm, between me and the world. The highest and coldest degree of the intransitivity of meaning, in which only an autistic responsorial chant occurs - weightless, without peace.

Poetic language is the wait for a word without us. It is language without empire, without home.

The living have no importance in poetic language. Poetic language is indifferent to the living.

Poetic language forgets us, has always forgotten us. It forgot us without wonder, without depth, without eternity. We are its sacrifice; left to talk while we die.

Poetic language is an act of inferiority. Makes us breathless.

Poetic language is a servile work.

Poetic language is an exercise in agony.

Poetic language is an exercise in sacrifice.

Poetic language is an exercise against reality.

Poetic language is an exercise against memory.

Poetic language is an exercise against immortality.

Poetic language is an exercise against poetry.

Because poetry is melodramatic, mystical, spiteful in the end.
It laughs infinitely at us. It seizes us and wondrously it kills us.

—vito m. bonito, translated by Allison Grimaldi Donahue

Translator's Note

Translating *Soffiati Via* has been a fully immersive experience. I do believe as translators we are capable of translating nearly anything if asked, but when we choose something to translate ourselves, we somehow also choose to live it ourselves. I began translating the work of vito m. bonito one poem at a time during the early morning hours in the winter of 2016. I was teaching high school at the time and would wake up and translate before the sun had come up, in the dark, under the lamplight. That early morning hour and the cool, cold darkness allowed me to inhabit the language of *Soffiati via* more fully, to wear it as a cloak of my own.

Bonito's language in this book is precise and ethereal and requires the reader to abandon any sense of security or surefootedness. The poems, made of short lines in short stanzas, build a completely new vocabulary for whomever is willing to enter this world. At first read the poems create images, but like all real poetry, they change the nature of how we understand those images through the very way in which their language operates. Bonito builds a world where suppressed voices find power, where what is stifled finds air, and the language for doing this work is newly found, original. Bonito changes the use of language, changes how verbs are used, how antiquated terms are granted meaning in a new context, and at times creates neologisms to help us understand a world that we, the living, know so little about.

Translating these poems underlines the problem of translating any poetry, the delicate question of entering into the mind and language of another human being. In this case the translation was particularly challenging because Bonito himself was writing in a highly performative voice, a voice that, as he points out in his essay here, is that of a serial killer, or a non-living child, in any case, of another realm and reality. Bonito's poems grant the English language new aesthetic freedom and room for possibility and out of the destruction that is translation comes new language and life.

—Allison Grimaldi Donahue
September 2020

About the Author

vito m. bonito has published books of poetry including *scatola cranica I-II* (Derbauch, 2021), *papaveri per niente* (Derbauch, 2021), *di non sapere infine a memoria 1978-1980* (L'Arcolaio, 2021), *fabula rasa* (Oèdipus, 2018), *la bambina bianca* (Derbauch, 2017), *Luce eterna* (Galerie Bordas Venezia, 2012), *Fioritura del sangue* (Perrone, 2010), *Sidereus Nuncius* (Grafiche Fioroni, 2009), *La vita inferiore* (Donzelli, 2004), *Campo degli orfani* (Book, 2000), *A distanza di neve* (Book, 1997). He has also written criticism featured in *Le parole e le ore. Gli orologi barocchi: antologia poetica del Seicento* (Sellerio, 1996), *L'occhio del tempo. L'orologio barocco tra letteratura, scienza ed emblematica* (Clueb, 1995), *Il gelo e lo sguardo. La poesia di Cosimo Ortesta e Valerio Magrelli* (Clueb, 1996), *Il canto della crisalide. Poesia e orfanità* (Clueb, 1999), *Pascoli*, (Liguori, 2007). He has written various essays on Montale, Beckett, Artaud, De Signoribus, Aristakisjan, the Coen brothers, Harmony Korine, Werner Herzog, and Socìetas Raffaello Sanzio. He teaches Italian literature in Bologna.

About the Translator

Allison Grimaldi Donahue is the author of *Body to Mineral* (Publication Studio Vancouver, 2016), the co-author of *On Endings* (Delere Press, 2019) and translator of *Self-portrait* by Carla Lonzi (Divided Publishing, 2021). Her writing and translations have appeared in *Prairie Schooner, Los Angeles Review of Books, Words Without Borders, The Massachusetts Review, BOMB, NERO* and *Tripwire*, and her performances have been presented in Italy at Gavin Brown's enterprise, MAMbo, MACRO and Short Theatre. She is a 2021–22 resident of Sommerakademie Paul Klee, Bern. She is Translations Editor at Hunger Mountain Review and lives in Bologna.

More poetry from Fomite...

Anna Blackmer — *Hexagrams*
L. Brown — *Loopholes*
Sue D. Burton — *Little Steel*
Christine Butterworth-McDermott — *Evelyn As*
David Cavanagh— *Cycling in Plato's Cave*
James Connolly — *Picking Up the Bodies*
Greg Delanty — *Loosestrife*
Mason Drukman — *Drawing on Life*
J. C. Ellefson — *Foreign Tales of Exemplum and Woe*
Anna Faktorovich — *Improvisational Arguments*
Barry Goldensohn — *Snake in the Spine, Wolf in the Heart*
Barry Goldensohn — *The Hundred Yard Dash Man*
Barry Goldensohn — *The Listener Aspires to the Condition of Music*
Barry Goldensohn — *Visitors Entrance*
R. L. Green — *When You Remember Deir Yassin*
KJ Hannah Greenberg — *Beast There—Don't That*
Gail Holst-Warhaft — *Lucky Country*
Judith Kerman — *Definitions*
Joseph Lamport — *Enlightenment*
Raymond Luczak — *A Babble of Objects*
Kate Magill — *Roadworthy Creature, Roadworthy Craft*
Tony Magistrale — *Entanglements*
Gary Mesick — *General Discharge*
Giorgio Mobili — *Sunken Boulevards*
Andreas Nolte — *Mascha: The Poems of Mascha Kaléko*
Sherry Olson — *Four-Way Stop*
Brett Ortler — *Lessons of the Dead*
David Polk — *Drinking the River*
Janice Miller Potter — *Meanwell*
Janice Miller Potter — *Thoreau's Umbrella*
Philip Ramp — *Arrivals and Departures*
Philip Ramp — *The Melancholy of a Life as the Joy of Living It Slowly Chills*
Joseph D. Reich — *A Case Study of Werewolves*
Joseph D. Reich — *Connecting the Dots to Shangrila*
Joseph D. Reich — *The Derivation of Cowboys and Indians*
Joseph D. Reich — *The Hole That Runs Through Utopia*
Joseph D. Reich — *The Housing Market*
Kenneth Rosen and Richard Wilson — *Gomorrah*
Fred Rosenblum — *Playing Chicken with an Iron Horse*
Fred Rosenblum — *Tramping Solo*
Fred Rosenblum — *Vietnumb*
David Schein — *My Murder and Other Local News*
Harold Schweizer — *Miriam's Book*
Scott T. Starbuck — *Carbonfish Blues*
Scott T. Starbuck — *Hawk on Wire*

Scott T. Starbuck — *Industrial Oz*
Seth Steinzor — *Among the Lost*
Seth Steinzor — *Once Was Lost*
Seth Steinzor — *To Join the Lost*
Susan Thomas — *In the Sadness Museum*
Susan Thomas — *Silent Acts of Public Indiscretion*
Susan Thomas — *The Empty Notebook Interrogates Itself*
Sharon Webster — *Everyone Lives Here*
Tony Whedon — *The Très Riches Heures*
Tony Whedon — *The Falkland Quartet*
Claire Zoghb — *Dispatches from Everest*

Dual Language
vito m. bonito/Allison Grimaldi Donahue — *Soffiata Via/Blown Away*
Antonello Borra/Blossom Kirschenbaum — *Alfabestiario*
Antonello Borra/Blossom Kirschenbaum — *AlphaBetaBestiario*
Antonello Borra/Anis Memon — *Fabbrica delle idee/The Factory of Ideas*
Tina Escaja/Mark Eisner — *Caída Libre/Free Fall*
Luigi Fontanella/Giorgio Mobili — *L'adolescenza e la notte/Adolescence and Night*
Giorgio Mobili — *Sunken Boulevards*
Aristea Papalexandrou/Philip Ramp — *Μας προσπερνά/It's Overtaking Us*
Katerina Anghelaki-Rooke//Philip Ramp — *Losing Appetite for Existence*
Jeannette Clariond/Lawrence Schimel — *Desert Memory*
Mikis Theodoraksi/Gail Holst-Warhaft — *The House with the Scorpions*
Paolo Valesio/Todd Portnowitz — *La Mezzanotte di Spoleto/Midnight in Spoleto*

Writing a review on social media sites for readers will help the progress of independent publishing. To submit a review, go to the book page on any of the sites and follow the links for reviews. Books from independent presses rely on reader-to-reader communications.

For more information or to order any of our books, visit:
http://www.fomitepress.com/our-books.html

www.ingramcontent.com/pod-product-compliance
Lightning Source LLC
Chambersburg PA
CBHW021427070526
44577CB00001B/92